Keystone Species that Live in the Mountains

Keystone Species in Nature

BONNIE HINMAN

Mitchell Lane
PUBLISHERS
P.O. Box 196
Hockessin, DE 19707
www.mitchelllane.com

PUBLISHERS

Printing   1   2   3   4   5   6   7   8

Keystone Species that Live in Deserts
Keystone Species that Live in Forests
Keystone Species that Live in Grasslands
Keystone Species that Live in Ponds, Streams, and Wetlands
Keystone Species that Live in the Mountains
Keystone Species that Live in the Sea and Along the Coastline

Library of Congress Cataloging-in-Publication Data
Hinman, Bonnie.
 Keystone species that live in the mountains / by Bonnie Hinman.
     pages cm. — (A kid's guide to keystone species in nature)
 Includes bibliographical references and index.
 Audience: Ages 8 to 11.
 Audience: Grades 3 to 6.
 ISBN 978-1-68020-060-7 (library bound)
 1. Keystone species—Juvenile literature. 2. Mountain ecology—Juvenile literature. I. Title.
 QH541.15.K48H56 2015
 577.5'3—dc23
                                                                    2015003172
eBook ISBN: 978-1-68020-061-4

PBP

Contents

Words in **bold** throughout can be found in the Glossary.

Introduction

Most arches built today contain a single building block at the top that is the most important piece. This special piece can be found in the arches of soaring cathedrals, doorways in temples, and even simple buildings made out of wooden blocks. It is called a keystone, and it holds everything else together. Remove the keystone and the building or doorway is likely to collapse.

The same thing is true in nature. Certain species of animals and plants are so important to their **ecosystems**, that if they disappear, the whole system may collapse. They are called keystone species.

Some keystone species are large, like mountain tapirs, while others are quite small, like red-naped sapsuckers. But size doesn't matter in an ecosystem. All living things

A keystone of a palace archway

Red-naped sapsucker

rely on other species to survive. A keystone species plays an especially large role that affects many different species in an ecosystem. Some keystone species are at the top of a huge ecosystem like the Greater Yellowstone Ecosystem, while others may affect a tiny ecosystem in a river or forest. Whether the ecosystem is big or small, the result of a keystone species disappearing or being greatly reduced is the same. Just like one falling domino can cause many others to fall, the loss of a keystone species can lead to the extinction of many other species.

Today scientists are focusing more attention on preserving the natural balance in ecosystems. Identifying and protecting keystone species is an important part of their work.

Chapter 1
SNOW LEOPARD

Ghosts roam the high mountains of Central Asia. Ghost *cats* that is. Snow leopards were given that nickname because they are hard to find in the wild. They hide from people[1] and they also blend into the rocky, snowy landscape.

Snow leopards have thick light gray to dark gray fur on most of their bodies, but their bellies are white. Grayish or blurred black spots cover their heads, necks, and legs. Rosettes, which are large rings that enclose smaller spots, cover the rest of their bodies. Their spots and colors provide them with **camouflage**.

Camouflage is important to snow leopards so they can sneak up on their prey. They jump as far as fifty feet (fifteen meters) in a single leap to ambush a blue sheep, Asiatic (ey-zhee-AT-ik) ibex, marmot, hare, or other animal that they like to eat.[2]

Snow leopards live in the mountains of twelve different countries including Afghanistan, Bhutan, Nepal, India, Russia, and China. They have a **range** of about eight hundred thousand square miles (two million square kilometers) spread across those twelve countries. That area is about the size of Mexico. Since there are only

Wildlife photographers have a hard time capturing a clear picture of a snow leopard in the wild. Besides having coats that blend into the mountain background, snow leopards are most active at night, dusk, and dawn. Since they are usually alone and secretive, snapping a picture of one can take days or even weeks.

an estimated 4,080 to 6,500 snow leopards left in the wild,[3] it is no wonder that scientists have a hard time finding them.

The snow leopard is an apex predator, which means that he is at the top of the food chain in his ecosystem. He has no natural enemies in the Himalayas and other mountain ranges spread throughout Central Asia.

The animals that the snow leopard hunts and eats are herbivores (HUR-buh-vawrs), or plant-eaters. Those herbivores, like sheep and ibex, would live longer if there were no snow leopards to kill them. Over time, there would be larger numbers of herbivores, who would eat more grass and plants. There would eventually be fewer grasses and plants for the sheep, ibex, and other herbivores to eat. Birds and small mammals who use the plants as homes and hiding places would suffer, too. Some species might even become extinct if snow leopards were not around.

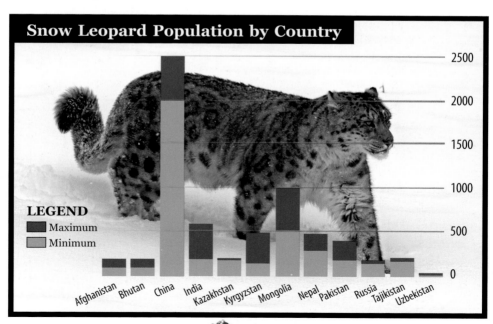

Snow Leopard Population by Country

LEGEND
- Maximum
- Minimum

Afghanistan, Bhutan, China, India, Kazakhstan, Kyrgyzstan, Mongolia, Nepal, Pakistan, Russia, Tajikistan, Uzbekistan

Built for the Mountains

Snow leopards are large cats. Most adults are about 77 to 121 pounds (35 to 55 kilograms) although a few will be heavier or lighter. Their bodies are usually 39 to 51 inches (100 to 130 centimeters) long. Their tails are almost as long as their bodies. A snow leopard's fat and furry tail helps him balance on the rocky ledges where he lives. The tail also helps keep in the warmth in cold weather. A snow leopard often curls his tail around his legs and face when he sleeps in the snow.

A snow leopard's feet are big for his size. His big paws help him walk on snow without sinking into it, just like snowshoes. They have fur and thick padding to protect him from the cold ground and sharp rocks. Because their bodies are built for cold, snowy environments, snow leopards feel right at home in the Central Asian mountains.

A snow leopard takes a nap on a rocky ledge. Cold temperatures do not bother snow leopards. They have fur that can be up to three inches long. Underneath that fur, they also have a thick layer of shorter, woolly fur.

Behavior and Babies

Snow leopards do not roar like other big cats. When they greet each other, they make quiet **chuffing** sounds with their noses. When a female is trying to find a mate, she makes a yowling sound.[4]

Snow leopards mate in the winter, and babies are born from 90 to 110 days later. Usually two or three cubs are born to the mother. The cubs are blind and helpless at birth. The mother allows them to follow her when they are about three months old. She teaches them to hunt, but they depend on her for food for at least another year. They are adults at about two years old.

This small snow leopard cub may have just begun to follow his mother as she hunts. The cubs remain in a hidden den until they are ready to follow Mom. The mother snow leopard returns to the den often to nurse her cubs. She also brings solid food to them after they are about two months old.

Snow leopards are **solitary** animals. They do not live in family groups. Only the mother and cubs will be together, except during mating season. Once the male and female mate, the male moves on. The female snow leopard raises her cubs by herself. She only has cubs every other year so she can teach the cubs to hunt during their first winter.

Snow leopards have large home ranges but they often overlap. Scientists believe that the sizes of the cats' home ranges depend on how much food is available in an area. They have smaller ranges when prey is plentiful and larger ranges when less prey is available.[5] They roam around their ranges all the time. Even though their ranges can overlap, snow leopards still keep their distance from one another. They leave markings to let other cats know where they are and warn them to stay away.

Humans: Harming or Helping?

Humans are the only enemies of snow leopards. Farmers and hunters who live in the mountains hunt them for several reasons. A snow leopard **pelt** is worth a lot of money in Asia. Sometimes hunters sell leopard bones and other body parts to make medicine. They may capture the leopards alive to sell them to zoos.

Farmers also kill snow leopards because the leopards sometimes kill the farmers' livestock. Snow leopards may not kill many of each farmer's animals, but even losing one animal is hard for them. And when the snow leopards get into livestock pens and kill several animals at once, the loss is even worse. This is a big deal to the herders and farmers in this region who typically only earn the equivalent of 250 to 400 US dollars each year.[6]

Another reason that snow leopards are endangered is that hunters kill the same animals the snow leopards like to eat. Herders' animals eat the same grasses that the wild sheep and ibex eat. So the wild animals have to move away to find food. This makes it harder for the snow leopards to find food in the area. Instead of eating the wild animals, the snow leopards eat farmers' livestock.

Conservation groups and some Asian governments are trying to protect snow leopards. It is not an easy job. These groups work to create laws that make hunting snow leopards illegal. But the laws alone are not enough. Governments also need to find and stop people who break those laws. The groups also try to find ways to help the herders and farmers so they won't need to kill the snow leopards.

One way to help is to provide better protection for the farmers' livestock. New stronger corrals keep livestock in and snow leopards out. But the best solution is for the snow leopards to have plenty of prey to eat in the wild. Then they can stop eating livestock. Herders are taught how they can manage their livestock so there will be grass left for the wild hoofed animals to eat. Governments also protect the snow leopards' prey from hunters with new laws. It remains to be seen whether these changes will be enough to save the snow leopard.

Snow leopards are important members of their high mountain ecosystem. Without these beautiful animals gliding through the mountains, many other species would suffer. Snow leopards face many challenges, but if people work together, we can keep them around for many years to come.

Born Helpless or Ready To Roam?

Some animal babies are so helpless when they hatch or are born that they would die quickly without the care and protection their parents give them. These are called altricial (al-TRISH-uhl) animals. Robins and kangaroos are altricial. Animals that are born or hatch with their eyes open and can walk soon after birth are called precocial (pri-KOH-shuhl) animals. Duck and elk babies are precocial.

Whether a species is altricial or precocial depends on where the mother gives birth. If her babies are altricial, she needs to find a protected place to keep her babies safe from predators. If she can't find a place like this in her environment, her altricial babies will quickly become another animal's dinner. Only precocial babies, who can stand and run from predators right away, can survive without a hiding place. The survival of all species depends on the survival of at least some of their babies. Nature makes sure that babies of every species have what they need to become adults.

Chapter 2

RED-NAPED SAPSUCKER

It might be better to call the red-naped sapsucker a "sapsipper" or even a "saplicker." He has a long pointed beak that he uses to get sap from a hole he makes in a tree. He doesn't really suck it out. His beak isn't like a straw. He sips or licks the sap with his tongue.

Tree sap is the liquid that flows just under the bark of a tree. It carries **nutrients** from the roots of a tree to its other parts. A tree usually has plenty of sap to spare. That's a good thing since many birds and insects love to eat sap. Humans eat tree sap, too. The sap from a maple tree is used to make maple syrup.

Sapsuckers belong to the woodpecker family. There are four species of sapsuckers, and three of them look very much alike. Until recently, scientists believed the yellow-bellied sapsucker, the red-breasted sapsucker, and the red-naped sapsucker were all a single species. Research proved that they are actually three different species.[1]

A red-naped sapsucker is from 7.5 to 9 inches (19 to 23 centimeters) long and has off-white and black feathers. Male birds have a red crown, **nape** patch, and throat patch. A female's lower throat is red and her chin

This red-naped sapsucker has tiny hairs on the tip of his tongue. After the bird drills a hole in the tree bark, he uses the hairs to pick up sap from the tree. The hairs collect sap much like the bristles of a paintbrush pick up paint.

is white, but she does not have a red nape patch. All young red-naped sapsuckers are a dull brown color.

Red-naped sapsuckers live in a large range in western North America. In the late spring and summer, the birds live in the Rocky Mountains from the United States to Canada. When winter comes, they migrate south to Mexico and the southwestern United States.

Drilling Holes: Food and Nests

A red-naped sapsucker's favorite meal is willow sap. They will eat sap from other trees, too, but they like willow best. They drill a series of tiny holes called sap wells in the bark of willow trees. The sap slowly seeps out of the holes. Sapsuckers are the first to eat at the wells but not the last. Hummingbirds, warblers, chipmunks, squirrels, wasps, butterflies, and other insects all eat sap from the wells. Scientists say that as many as forty species feed from these holes.[2]

Sapsuckers like to make their homes by drilling nesting **cavities** in aspen trees. Aspen wood is soft, but some aspen trees are softer than others. When shelf **fungus** begins to grow on an aspen, it causes the tree's trunk to rot. This is bad news for the aspen, but good news for red-naped sapsuckers. After the fungus has softened the wood, the sapsucker can drill through more easily. It's not surprising that the sapsuckers prefer to make their homes in these softened trees, when they have a choice.[3]

Family Life

Male and female red-naped sapsuckers have a **courtship** display. They swoop and glide near each other and drum on trees with their beaks. Once they have agreed to build

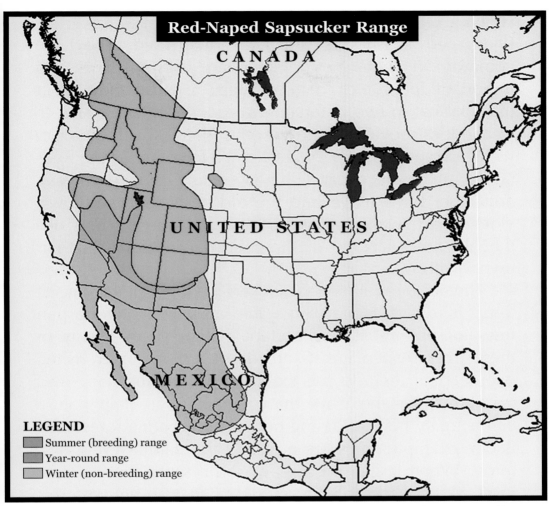

Red-Naped Sapsucker Range

CANADA

UNITED STATES

MEXICO

LEGEND
Summer (breeding) range
Year-round range
Winter (non-breeding) range

a nest, they both **excavate** the nesting cavity. They usually choose a location for their nest that is near water and willow trees.

The female lays four or five eggs in the nest, and the pair take turns sitting on the eggs. In about two weeks the eggs hatch. The babies are blind and don't have any feathers. Both parents tend to the chicks and they grow quickly. The young birds first leave the nest when they are about a month old.[4] Their parents teach them to drill holes to find sap. After a few days, they are on their own.

Helping Other Birds

Red-naped sapsuckers are not endangered. They are common in their North American **habitat**. It is still important to protect them, though, because they affect their habitat in two different ways.

Besides providing food for other species with their sap wells, sapsuckers also create homes for other birds. Red-naped sapsuckers excavate a new nesting cavity each year, and other birds move into the old nests. Tree swallows, violet-green swallows, chickadees, and house wrens use the old holes.[5] None of these birds can excavate their own cavities.

Threats to red-naped sapsuckers are few, but the biggest threat is loss of habitat. Since the sapsuckers prefer aspen trees for nesting, it is important that there are plenty of these trees. Aspen forests are destroyed, however, when people clear them to use the land for building.

Sometimes the ways that people try to help nature can actually hurt it. Putting out and preventing forest fires is one example. Fires are a part of the natural cycle of a forest. When large, old trees live in a forest, young trees can't get enough sunlight to grow.[6] Fires can help a forest by killing the old trees, making room for young aspens.

If aspen trees disappear from an area, the red-naped sapsuckers would move away. Then the birds, insects, and mammals that depend on sapsucker wells and nesting cavities would move as well. Or they might die off.

There are plenty of red-naped sapsuckers right now, but if something happened to them or their habitat, many other species could be gone forever. Nature has many ways of keeping its systems in balance, but sometimes humans disturb that balance, affecting everyone.

Why Do Birds Migrate?

It seems like birds could save themselves a lot of trouble if they just stayed in one place all year. Some birds do stay put, but others migrate or move from one location to another during the spring and fall. Food and raising babies are the two biggest reasons birds migrate. Birds fly to cooler areas away from the equator in the spring because there is a rich new crop of insects and plants to eat. But when those plants and insects start to disappear in the fall, they head to the warmer, tropical regions. Birds can't raise their babies, there, though. The heat could be dangerous for newborn chicks. So when spring comes, they return to the cooler regions to make their nests and prepare to care for their young.

Chapter 3
GRAY WOLF

Are wolves big and bad? Or are they wild creatures who want to be left alone? Fairy tales, movies, and books tell us both stories. Until recently most people only wanted to get rid of wolves. But are they really so bad?

Although it is very rare, wolves can attack humans. A wolf might attack if a person gets between a mother wolf and her pup. Wolves also kill and eat livestock. Ranchers and herders around the world have killed wolves for that reason.

Wolves would rather eat an elk or deer than a cow or sheep, however. If there are other animals for a wolf to eat, a gray wolf is happy to stay away from people and their livestock. A wolf does not want to be around people unless it thinks it has to protect a pup or find something to eat.

There are two wolf species: the gray wolf and the red wolf. Most wolves in the world are subspecies of the gray wolf. There are five subspecies of gray wolves in North America and at least seven in Europe and Asia.[1]

Many years ago gray wolves lived in more places in the world than any other mammal. They were common in such countries as Ireland, Japan, and Switzerland where

An alpha wolf looks for prey on a winter day. He will lead his pack as far as twelve miles (twenty kilometers) in one day on a hunting trip. If the pack is lucky enough to find a big elk or moose, they will eat as much as possible. One wolf can eat twenty pounds (nine kilograms) of meat at one time.

they are now **regionally extinct**. Gray wolves still live in many countries including Bulgaria, Germany, Finland, Latvia, Ukraine, and the United States.[2]

Gray Wolf Appearance and Habitat

Gray wolves look a lot like German shepherds but there are many differences. Wolves have longer muzzles and most adults have yellow eyes. Their legs are longer with larger paws. The teeth of a wolf are also bigger than a dog's teeth. A gray wolf's color can range from all white to white with a little brown or gray to mostly black.

Adult gray wolves range from 50 to 130 pounds (23 to 59 kilograms), although in some places, they can be as small as 30 pounds (14 kilograms) or as heavy as 175 pounds (79 kilograms). From the tip of their nose to the tip of their tail, they are typically 54 to 78 inches (137 to 198 centimeters) long. Gray wolves are about 26 to 32 inches (66 to 81 centimeters) tall at their shoulders.[3] Males are usually larger than females.

Gray wolves prefer to live in remote areas but can live almost anywhere there is plenty of food. They live in deserts, **tundra**, mountains, and grasslands. A large population of gray wolves lives in the Carpathian Mountains in Central and Eastern Europe. This is a good place for wolves because fewer people live there than in surrounding areas.[4]

A gray wolf's favorite meal is a big-hoofed mammal like a moose, caribou, or bison. However, they will also eat rabbits, mice, snakes, and birds. A bison or moose is a lot bigger than a wolf so wolves have to work together to bring down one of these animals.

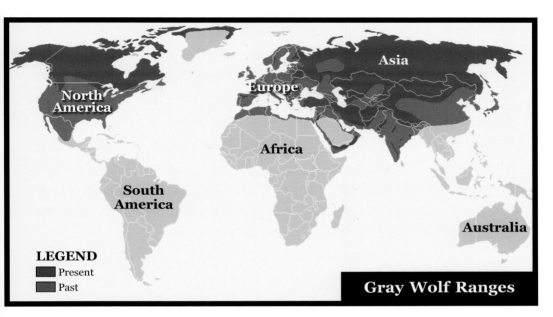

LEGEND
■ Present
■ Past

Gray Wolf Ranges

Life in the Wolf Pack

Wolves live with their families in groups called packs. Usually a wolf pack includes a male and female and their pups. Sometimes an older female or one or two unrelated males may also be pack members. Packs usually have four to nine wolves, but a pack of twenty or more wolves is not uncommon.

Gray wolf packs have a rank order. This means that some members are considered more important than others by the pack. The male and female parents are the alpha pair. They are at the top of the rank order. Either the male or female might be the leader of the pack. Each of the other pack members has a lower rank in the pack.

The alpha pair may decide when to hunt or where to rest, but they don't always make those decisions. Their position at the top of the pack means that they can do what they want any time they want. The other wolves follow along if they want to, but they don't have to.[5]

Gray wolves mate in late winter so their pups can be born after the worst of winter weather is over. Pups are born in the spring or early summer after a **gestation** period of about two months. The average **litter** size is six or seven pups. The babies are born blind and deaf. They depend on their mother for warmth and she also provides them with food by nursing them. During the first three weeks, a wolf mother stays with her pups almost all of the time. Other pack members bring meat to the mother and provide protection for the den.

Pups grow quickly and first go outside the den sometime after they are three weeks old. From that time, all members of the pack take care of the pups until they are grown. By about four to five weeks old, they eat **regurgitated** food that their mother or other pack members

Wolf pups practice howling just like they practice hunting. Wolves use howls, whines, growls, and barks to communicate with each other. Pups do a lot of yapping, too, but they soon learn to howl properly by imitating the adult wolves.

bring to them. After the pups are around forty-five days old, they eat regular meat provided to them by the pack members.[6]

Wolf pups play games much like those that human children play. They play keep-away, tag, wrestling, and king-of-the-mountain. These games are fun for the pups but also help them develop skills they need to survive.[7]

At about four to eight months old, the pups begin to follow the pack on hunting trips. Some pups leave to form their own pack or family by the time they are only nine or ten months old. But many pups of both genders live with their parents until they are three years old, or sometimes older.

Saving Wolves

People around the world have tried to get rid of wolves for hundreds of years. The wolves were poisoned, trapped, and shot. Wolves almost became extinct in the early twentieth century in the United States and Western Europe. It was not until the 1960s and 1970s that scientists and conservationists all over the world began trying to save the gray wolf from extinction. People were starting to see just how important wolves are to their ecosystem.

The communities of prey are stronger and healthier when wolves are around. That's because wolves eat the animals that are the easiest to catch. Those animals are usually weak, old, hurt, or sick. The strongest and healthiest prey animals are able to outrun or fight off the wolves. Wolves also help to keep prey populations from growing too large. This saves their habitat from overgrazing. The plants are able to remain healthy and continue growing when there are fewer herbivores.

A wolf pack chases a bull elk in Yellowstone National Park. Their next move may be to slash its hind leg tendons to bring it down. Sometimes the pack will herd the animal back toward the rest of the pack members before killing it. A healthy adult elk can defend itself against a pack of wolves, but a sick or old one is probably doomed.

Wolf conservation efforts have been successful in many places. From 1914 to 1926, the wolves were killed in Yellowstone National Park in the northwestern United States. By the early 1990s, the elk population had grown too large. They were eating so many tree leaves and branches that many of the trees were dying. Other animals that depend on the trees, like birds and beavers, had moved to other areas. Since that time, scientists have brought wolves back to Yellowstone National Park, which has helped restore the natural balance in the park.[8]

Worldwide, people are the biggest threat to wolves. Even though there are ways to keep livestock safe from wolves, people still fear wolves and want to kill them. People also build homes and businesses in wolves' habitat areas. This forces wolves to live closer to populated areas and causes more conflict. It is important for people to find a way to live with wolves or they may vanish forever from our lands.

Wolfdogs

Wolfdogs are also called wolf **hybrids**. Their parents are a wolf and a dog. People sometimes buy wolfdogs because they think that they would make great pets. While wolves and dogs have the same **ancestors**, they are now very different. Wolves are still wild animals, while dogs have lived with people for thousands of years. Many wolfdog buyers think they are getting an animal that looks like a wolf but acts like a dog. But it is very hard to predict which traits a wolfdog will inherit from each of its parents. A wolfdog may try to challenge its owner to become the leader of the pack. This is normal for a wolf but not for a dog. Many people end up giving their wolfdog away or setting it free because they cannot train or take care of the animal.[9]

Chapter 4
MOUNTAIN TAPIR

A mountain tapir (TEY-per) looks like a long-legged pig with a short trunk. He also has a wooly coat that a pig would love to have in the winter. In spite of his appearance the mountain tapir is more closely related to a horse or a rhino than a pig.

Animals like tapirs show up in fossil records from fifty to sixty million years ago. Some scientists call the tapir a living fossil because it looks about the same today as it did twenty million years ago.[1]

Aside from mountain tapirs, there are four other kinds of tapirs in the world. Brazilian or lowland tapirs along with Baird's tapirs live in South and Central America on lower land than the mountain tapir. They do not have wooly coats. The Malayan (muh-LEY-uhn) tapir lives in Southeast Asia and is the biggest of the five.

The fifth tapir species is a brand new discovery. The kabomani tapir was officially named a separate species in 2013. The kabomani tapir is smaller than the other four species, and it lives in the Amazon rainforest in Brazil and Colombia.[2]

Mountain tapirs are the only tapirs to live high in the mountains. They are found in the Andes Mountains

For all their bulk, mountain tapirs are good climbers and can move quickly to escape threats. They have three toes on each of their back feet and four on their front feet. The smaller fourth toe on the front foot normally does not touch the ground, except when the tapir walks on soft land or mud.

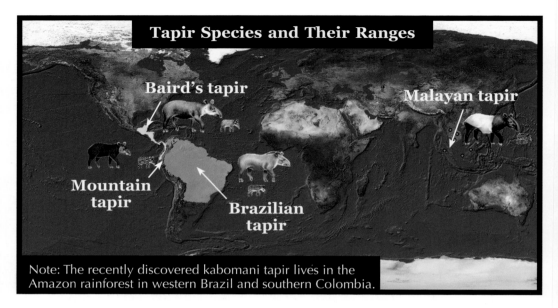

Tapir Species and Their Ranges

Baird's tapir

Malayan tapir

Mountain tapir

Brazilian tapir

Note: The recently discovered kabomani tapir lives in the Amazon rainforest in western Brazil and southern Colombia.

of Peru, Ecuador, and Colombia. Their reddish-brown to black fur coat is an inch (2.5 centimeters) long with a thick undercoat. They need protection from the cold night temperatures in the mountains.[3]

If you have seen a mountain tapir's nose, it should be no surprise that a mountain tapir has a great sense of smell. But the tapir's nose and upper lip combine to form a **snout** that is used for more than just smelling. A tapir can use his snout like fingers to grasp leaves or fruit and put the food right into his mouth.

Mountain tapirs are about 6 feet (1.8 meters) long and weigh from 330 to 550 pounds (150 to 250 kilograms).[4] Females are a little bit bigger than males. A tapir's front feet have four toes, but the back feet have three toes.

The Life of a Mountain Tapir

Mating season for mountain tapirs is right before the beginning of the rainy season. Males often fight over females. Males and females make wheezing or whistling sounds during the courtship period. After mating, many males go back to living by themselves. Occasionally, a male may stay with the same female for life.

The gestation time for mountain tapirs is thirteen months. Because their pregnancy is so long, females only give birth every other year, early in the rainy season. Twins are rarely born so the population of mountain tapirs grows very slowly.

Newborn mountain tapirs have yellow and white stripes and spots. This provides them with camouflage, which later disappears when they are big enough to defend themselves. They weigh from 8 to 15 pounds (4 to 7 kilograms) at birth. The calves can stand within an hour or two after birth and in a week can follow their mothers. They nurse for about six months and stay with their mother for a year or more.[5]

Mountain tapirs are herbivores, and they will eat many different kinds of leaves and plants. But they do have favorites. They especially like to eat a type of flowering plant called *Lupinus*. A tree with silver-green leaves called *Gynoxys* comes in second on their list of favorite foods.[6]

Mountain tapir calf

Mountain tapirs are shy and will hide if startled. They usually live alone except when mothers have babies living with them. Scientists have discovered recently that small groups of tapirs may graze together. They are territorial and do not like to find another tapir in their home range even though the territories sometimes overlap. If they get into a fight over their territory, they can use their sharp teeth to hurt each other.

Early morning and right before dark are the times that mountain tapirs are most active. They push through trees, eating as they go. During the middle of the day, they like to rest hidden under thick plants or—better yet—swim. Swimming is a mountain tapir's favorite thing to do when

A mountain tapir takes a relaxing dip in a cool pool on a hot afternoon. Mountain tapirs also head for water sometimes to escape predators. If the water hole dries up, tapirs like to wallow in mud. A nice coat of mud on their skin protects them from insect bites.

it gets hot in the mountains. Tapirs are excellent swimmers and they raise their snouts above the water and breathe as if they had snorkels. This helps them hide from hunters or predators.

Planting Seeds

Mountain tapirs are excellent seed **dispersers**, but they do not do this on purpose. They just like to eat fruit, berries, and grasses, along with the seeds they contain. Some of the seeds pass through the tapirs' digestive systems and come out as waste. This process could take up to ten days, and the tapir can travel a long distance in this time. When the seeds come out, they land on the ground inside a pile of poop, which acts like **fertilizer**. Some of the seeds will sprout and grow into new plants, often far away from their parent plant.

Many other animals depend on the plants that grow from the seeds the tapir spreads. A good example is the Quindio wax palm tree. Scientists say that the wax palm may depend so much on the mountain tapir to spread its seeds that it could vanish if the tapir goes extinct. The wax palm tree provides food for birds and other animals. Parrots make their nests in the palms. If the wax palm cannot survive, then other animals may not either.[7]

Decreasing Numbers

Mountain tapirs are in real danger of becoming extinct. There are an estimated 2,500 of them left in the wild and that number is decreasing.[8] As with many endangered animals, people pose the greatest threat to the tapirs. As more people move into the mountain areas, they cut down trees and plants to make room for their buildings

These spindly Quindio wax palm trees can grow as tall as 164 to 196 feet (50 to 60 meters). They live in the Cocora Valley in Colombia. Wax palm trees can live 120 years. The wax on their trunks was used to make candles and soap until the trees were protected under Colombian law.

and farms. This could eventually leave the tapirs with no good place to live.

Hunting by **poachers** also hurts the mountain tapir. In Colombia people use tapir skin to make ropes, baskets, and backpacks. Others use the tapir's skin and feet for medicine. Mountain tapirs have so few babies that they cannot survive if humans keep killing them and destroying their homes.[9]

Mountain tapirs have lived in South America for millions of years. They are more than just animals with funny-looking noses and furry skin; they are an important part of their ecosystem. Whether they survive another million years will be up to humans to decide.

What Are Fossils?

Fossils are the remains or impressions of plants or animals that lived thousands, millions, or even billions of years ago. A fossil can be the actual bones, shells, or wood of an animal or plant. It can also be the impression left behind by a plant or animal that once lived. A leaf that fell to the ground ten thousand years ago might be pressed between layers of rock. The leaf itself disappeared but the impression it left behind is still there in the rock. It is rare to find a fossil that has skin or hair preserved. If an animal or a man fell into something that quickly hardened around him or was very cold, the soft tissues could survive. But only a few of these fossils have ever been found.

Chapter 5

WHITEBARK PINE

A keystone species does not have to be able to run, swim, hop, crawl, or fly to do its important job. A whitebark pine tree stands still in its landscape, except when the wind blows through its branches. Yet it is so important to other plants, animals, and birds, that if it becomes extinct, these other species will also suffer.

Whitebark pines belong to a group of trees called stone pines. There are five kinds of stone pine trees in the world. They're called stone pines because their seeds are heavy like stones. The whitebark lives in the western United States and Canada. They are found in several different mountain ranges including the Rocky Mountains, Cascade Range, and Sierra Nevada.

Some scientists believe that whitebark pine seeds came to North America more than 1.8 million years ago. The ancestors of birds called Clark's nutcrackers may have carried the seeds of the ancestors of the whitebark pines across the Bering land bridge.[1] This narrow stretch of land connected Asia and North America millions of years ago before it was covered by water. When they first arrived, the pines lived throughout North America. The climate began to warm about eight thousand years ago, however.

This multiple-trunk whitebark pine tree lives in the Copper Mountains in northeastern Nevada. A tree this size could be 250 to 300 years old. Whitebark pines have spreading roots that anchor into the rocky ground. These pines are seldom uprooted in spite of the violent winds that blow through the mountains.

Whitebark pines have only lived on the mountains since that time, because they need cold temperatures to grow.[2]

Whitebark pines grow slowly and live a long time. They can live to be five hundred to one thousand years old. A whitebark pine that sprouted before Columbus arrived in America could still be growing today.

Living High on the Mountain

How tall a whitebark pine gets depends on how high in the mountains it lives. A whitebark pine growing at a low **elevation** may grow to a height of fifty to sixty feet (fifteen to eighteen meters) by the time it is two hundred to three hundred years old. Even taller whitebarks have occasionally been found. When whitebarks grow at very high elevations, however, they are much shorter. Many whitebarks have multiple trunks, but the tallest trees can have a single trunk. The **crown** is often rounded, but the branches can sometimes spread in different directions. Trees that live highest on the mountains are **stunted** and look like shrubs. Groups of these stunted pines are called *krummholz* (KROOM-hohlts) stands.

Krummholz means "crooked wood" or "twisted wood" in German. Krummholz stands appear when trees are exposed to extreme cold temperatures and strong mountain winds. The trees twist as they grow to try to **adapt** to the conditions. They may also start new roots from any branches that touch the ground.

A Little Help from the Birds

Whitebark pines have needles that grow in bunches of five. These needles are a pine tree's leaves. Seeds for whitebark pine trees are contained in purple egg-shaped cones. The cones are two to three inches (four to eight centimeters) long and turn brown in late summer. Most pinecones ripen and open to release their seeds to the wind. But whitebark pinecones do not do this. They remain firmly closed until a bird or other animal cracks them open.

The closed cones mean that whitebark pines depend on other species to move their seeds away from the mother tree. Clark's nutcrackers and red squirrels do most of this work. They crack open the cones and take the seeds for food.

Clark's nutcrackers like to harvest many seeds and hide them to eat later. They hold seeds in their throat, and then bury them in an underground **cache** for storage. By the time the cones are all gone in the fall, the nutcrackers have caches of seeds everywhere. They store many more seeds than they can actually eat, so lots of seeds are still in the underground caches by springtime. When conditions are right, the seeds can germinate and grow into new whitebark pine trees.

Seeds for Supper

Red squirrels hide whitebark pine cones on the ground or in rotten logs. Grizzly bears and black bears search for these caches in the fall so they can fatten up before they hibernate. Whitebark seeds are high in fat, so they help the bears pile on the pounds quickly before winter sets in.

The Clark's nutcracker, red squirrel, and black and grizzly bears aren't the only species that depend on whitebark pines for their dinners. Other birds that eat the seeds include nuthatches, chickadees, woodpeckers, and pine grosbeaks. Ground squirrels and chipmunks eat the seeds, too.[3]

Whitebark pine forests provide food, shelter, and nest sites for many other species. Deer, elk, and snowshoe hares live among the trees in places that other trees can't grow. Migrating tropical birds stop to rest in the trees during their journeys to summer or winter homes.

Whitebark pines are ecosystem engineers. This means that they create or change habitats. One way they do this is by reducing soil erosion. A whitebark pine's roots pull water from the soil and hold the soil in place. Whitebark pines also produce shade, which keeps the snow from melting too quickly in the spring. If the trees were not there, the melting snow could flow down the mountains and cause flooding below. That would affect farms and even the drinking water supply. Because whitebark pines grow where other trees cannot, their ecosystem depends on them to do this.[4]

Protecting the Pines

Whitebark pines face several threats to their existence. In 2011 the US Fish and Wildlife Service announced that the whitebark pine needs protection. However, the agency decided that other species need to be protected first. The US government cannot do anything to help the whitebark pines until the species is added to the Federal List of Endangered and Threatened Wildlife and Plants.[5]

White pine blister rust is a tree disease that is killing many whitebark pines. Caused by a fungus, this disease came to North America by accident. It arrived in the United States with a shipment of trees from Europe in the early 1900s. By 1910, it had been introduced to

British Columbia, Canada. The disease was first seen in a whitebark pine in the 1920s. It has been killing whitebark pine trees ever since. Scientists have noticed that some trees don't get white pine blister rust. These trees seem to have a natural protection that was inherited from its parent tree. Conservation groups are working to find these trees and plant more of their seeds.

The mountain pine beetle lays its eggs under the bark of trees, which kills the trees quickly. The beetle is common throughout western North America. Chemical sprays can protect a tree from the beetles, but it isn't easy to treat so many trees. The chemicals could also cause more harm to the environment. Mountain pine beetles are killing more trees today than they were in the past because the climate is changing. Warmer temperatures allow the beetles to live longer, so there are more of them attacking the trees. Some forests have both white pine blister rust and mountain pine beetles.

Climate change doesn't only increase the number of mountain pine beetles. Whitebark pine trees love cold temperatures. As temperatures rise, the trees are at risk of dying. Less rain and snow could also hurt the trees' chances of survival.

The US Forest Service and other conservation groups have worked hard to stop forest fires. But occasional fires help whitebark pines. They do not like to grow in shade and a fire creates open space with lots of sun to grow in. They are often the first trees to grow again after a fire.

Many groups are trying to help the whitebark pine forests survive and grow. Sometimes it is hard to understand how important a single tree species can be in our world. But every species helps maintain nature's balance.

Ecosystem Engineers

Engineers build or change things. Animals and plants are called ecosystem engineers when they build or change the ecosystem where they live. Sometimes animals like beavers do this by moving things. A beaver cuts down trees and builds homes and dams. The dams make ponds. These new ponds become home to many other species. Some species like lianas (lee-AH-nuhz), which are woody vines, change their ecosystem by growing as they naturally do. Liana vines connect trees when they grow along the tops of forest canopies. Monkeys use the vines as pathways to travel from one place to another high up in the trees.[6]

beaver dam

CHAPTER NOTES

Chapter 1: Snow Leopard

1. Angie McPherson, "Rare Pictures: Snow Leopards Caught in Camera Trap," *National Geographic*, January 25, 2014, http://news.nationalgeographic.com/news/2014/01/140125-snow-leopard-pakistan-animals-science-world-endangered-species/
2. World Wildlife Foundation, "Snow Leopard," http://wwf.panda.org/what_we_do/endangered_species/snow_leopard/
3. Ibid.
4. Leah Montsion, "*Uncia uncia*: Snow Leopard," *Animal Diversity Web*, University of Michigan Museum of Zoology, 2014, http://animaldiversity.org/accounts/Uncia_uncia/
5. Snow Leopard Trust, "Habitat," http://www.snowleopard.org/learn/cat-facts/habitat
6. Snow Leopard Conservancy, "Threats To Snow Leopard Survival," http://snowleopardconservancy.org/threats-to-snow-leopard-survival/

Chapter 2: Red-Naped Sapsucker

1. Leo Shapiro, "*Sphyrapicus nuchalis*, Red-naped Sapsucker: Brief Summary," *Encyclopedia of Life*, http://eol.org/pages/1047045/details
2. Gretchen C. Daily, Paul R. Ehrlich, and Nick M. Haddad, "Double Keystone Bird in a Keystone Species Complex," *Proceedings of the National Academy of Sciences USA*, January 1993, p. 592, http://www.ncbi.nlm.nih.gov/pmc/articles/PMC45709/pdf/pnas01100-0238.pdf
3. G. Hammerson, "Red-Naped Sapsucker: Ecology & Life History," NatureServe Explorer, March 6, 2009, http://explorer.natureserve.org/servlet/NatureServe?searchName=Sphyrapicus+nuchalis
4. State of Utah Natural Resources, Division of Wildlife Resources, "Red-Naped Sapsucker," http://dwrcdc.nr.utah.gov/rsgis2/search/SearchSelection.asp?Group=AVES&Species=VERT
5. Daily, et al., "Double Keystone Bird in a Keystone Species Complex," pp. 592, 594.
6. G. Hammerson, "Red-Naped Sapsucker: Conservation Status," NatureServe Explorer, October 13, 1999, http://explorer.natureserve.org/servlet/NatureServe?searchName=Sphyrapicus+nuchalis

Chapter 3: Gray Wolf

1. International Wolf Center, "Wolf FAQs," January 2014, http://www.wolf.org/learn/basic-wolf-info/wolf-faqs/
2. L.D. Mech and L. Boitani, "*Canis lupus*," The IUCN Red List of Threatened Species, 2010, Version 2014.3, http://www.iucnredlist.org/details/3746/0
3. International Wolf Center, "Wolf FAQs."
4. Large Herbivore Network/ECNC, "Carpathians," http://www.lhnet.org/carpathians/
5. Wolf Park, "Wolves," http://wolfpark.org/animals/info/wolves/
6. Tanya Dewey and Julia Smith, "*Canis lupus*, Gray Wolf," *Animal Diversity Web*, University of Michigan Museum of Zoology, 2002, http://animaldiversity.org/accounts/Canis_lupus/
7. Jane M. Packard, "Wolf Behavior: Reproductive, Social, and Intelligent," in L. David Mech and Luigi Boitani, eds., *Wolves: Behavior, Ecology, and Conservation* (Chicago: The University of Chicago Press, 2003), pp. 49-50.
8. Douglas H. Chadwick, "Keystone Species: How Predators Create Abundance and Stability," *Mother Earth News*, June/July 2011, http://www.motherearthnews.com/nature-and-environment/keystone-species-zm0z11zrog.aspx
9. International Wolf Center, "Wolf-Dog Hybrids," http://www.wolf.org/learn/basic-wolf-info/wolves-and-humans/wolf-dog-hybrids/

Chapter 4: Mountain Tapir

1. Natalie Nechvatal, "*Tapirus pinchaque*: Mountain Tapir," *Animal Diversity Web*, University of Michigan Museum of Zoology, 2001, http://animaldiversity.org/accounts/Tapirus_pinchaque/
2. Darren Naish, "A New Living Species of Large Mammal: Hello, *Tapirus kabomani!*" *Scientific American*, December 17, 2013, http://blogs.scientificamerican.com/tetrapod-zoology/2013/12/17/new-living-species-of-tapir/
3. Natalie Nechvatal, "*Tapirus pinchaque*: Mountain Tapir."
4. IUCN/SSC Tapir Specialist Group, "The World's Tapirs—The Mountain Tapir (*Tapirus pinchaque*)," http://tapirs.org/tapirs/mountain.html
5. Natalie Nechvatal, "*Tapirus pinchaque*: Mountain Tapir."
6. Craig C. Downer, "Observations on the Diet and Habitat of the Mountain Tapir (*Tapirus pinchaque*)," *Journal of Zoology*, 2001, vol. 254, p. 284. http://tapiruscol.tripod.com/recursos/Downer2001.pdf
7. Ibid., p. 286.
8. A.G. Diaz, et al., "*Tapirus pinchaque*," The IUCN Red List of Threatened Species, Version 2014.2, June 30, 2008, http://www.iucnredlist.org/details/21473/0
9. Ibid.

CHAPTER NOTES

Chapter 5: Whitebark Pine

1. Taza Schaming, "Importance of Whitebark Pines and Clark's Nutcrackers in Western Ecosystems," *American Forests*, http://www.americanforests.org/our-programs/endangered-western-forests/importance-of-whitebark-pines-and-clarks-nutcrackers-in-western-ecosystems/

2. Aaron M. Ellison, et al., "Loss of Foundation Species: Consequences For the Structure and Dynamics of Forested Ecosystems," *Frontiers in Ecology and the Environment*, November 2005, p. 482. http://www.srs.fs.usda.gov/pubs/ja/ja_elliott019.pdf

3. Whitebark Pine Ecosystem Foundation, "Why Whitebark Pine Matters," http://whitebarkfound.org/?page_id=22

4. Ibid.

5. US Fish and Wildlife Service, "Whitebark Pine," Endangered Species: Mountain-Prairie Region, April 10, 2014, http://www.fws.gov/mountain-prairie/species/plants/whitebarkpine/

6. Paul D. Haemig, "Ecosystem Engineers: Organisms That Create, Modify and Maintain Habitats," Ecology.info, http://www.ecology.info/ecosystem-engineers.htm

WORKS CONSULTED

Andean Tapir Fund. "The Mountain Tapir." http://www.andeantapirfund.com/

Arno, Stephen F., and Raymond J. Hoff. "*Pinus albicaulis* Engelm.: Whitebark Pine." USDA Forest Service. http://www.na.fs.fed.us/pubs/silvics_manual/Volume_1/pinus/albicaulis.htm

BBC Nature. *Prehistoric Life.* "Fossils." http://www.bbc.co.uk/nature/fossils

Chadwick, Douglas H. "Keystone Species: How Predators Create Abundance and Stability." *Mother Earth News*, June/July 2011. http://www.motherearthnews.com/nature-and-environment/keystone-species-zm0z11zrog.aspx

------. "Out of the Shadows." *National Geographic*, June 2008. http://ngm.nationalgeographic.com/2008/06/snow-leopards/chadwick-text/4

Cornell Lab of Ornithology. *All About Birds.* "Red-Naped Sapsucker: Life History." http://www.allaboutbirds.org/guide/red-naped_sapsucker/lifehistory

Daily, Gretchen C., Paul R. Ehrlich, and Nick M. Haddad. "Double Keystone Bird in a Keystone Species Complex." *Proceedings of the National Academy of Sciences USA*, January 1993, pp.592-594. http://www.ncbi.nlm.nih.gov/pmc/articles/PMC45709/pdf/pnas01100-0238.pdf

Dewey, Tanya, and Julia Smith. "*Canis lupus*, Gray Wolf." A*nimal Diversity Web*, University of Michigan Museum of Zoology, 2002. http://animaldiversity.org/accounts/Canis_lupus/

Diaz, A.G., A. Castellanos, C. Piñeda, C. Downer, D.J. Lizcano, E. Constantino, J.A. Suárez Mejía, J. Camancho, J. Darria, J. Amanzo, J. Sánchez, J. Sinisterra Santana, L. Ordoñez Delgado, L.A. Espino Castellanos, and O.L. Montenegro. "*Tapirus pinchaque*." The IUCN Red List of Threatened Species, Version 2014.2, 2008. http://www.iucnredlist.org/details/21473/0

Downer, Craig C. "Observations on the Diet and Habitat of the Mountain Tapir (*Tapirus pinchaque*)." *Journal of Zoology*, 2001, vol. 254, pp. 279-291. http://tapiruscol.tripod.com/recursos/Downer2001.pdf

Ellison, Aaron M., Michael S. Bank, Barton D. Clinton, Elizabeth A. Colburn, Katherine Elliott, Chelcy R. Ford, David R. Foster, Brian D. Kloeppel, Jennifer D. Knoepp, Gary M. Lovett, Jacqueline Mohan, David A. Orwig, Nicholas L. Rodenhouse, William V. Sobczak, Kristina A. Stinson, Jeffrey K. Stone, Christopher M. Swan, Jill Thompson, Betsy Von Holle, and Jackson R. Webster. "Loss of Foundation Species: Consequences For the Structure and Dynamics of Forested Ecosystems." *Frontiers in Ecology and the Environment*, November 2005, pp. 479-486. http://www.srs.fs.usda.gov/pubs/ja/ja_elliott019.pdf

Haemig, Paul D. "Ecosystem Engineers: Organisms That Create, Modify, and Maintain Habitats." Ecology.info. http://www.ecology.info/ecosystem-engineers.htm

Hammerson, G. "Red-Naped Sapsucker." NatureServe Explorer, March 6, 2009. http://explorer.natureserve.org/servlet/NatureServe?searchName= Sphyrapicus+nuchalis

International Wolf Center. "Wolf-Dog Hybrids." http://www.wolf.org/learn/basic-wolf-info/wolves-and-humans/wolf-dog-hybrids/

International Wolf Center. "Wolf FAQs." January 2014. http://www.wolf.org/learn/basic-wolf-info/wolf-faqs/#m

IUCN/SSC Tapir Specialist Group. "The World's Tapirs—The Mountain Tapir (*Tapirus pinchaque*)." http://tapirs.org/tapirs/mountain.html

Large Herbivore Network/ECNC. "Carpathians." http://www.lhnet.org/Carpathians/

------. "Gray Wolf—*Canis lupus*." http://www.lhnet.org/gray-wolf/

Mahalovich, M., and L. Stritch. "*Pinus albicaulis*." The IUCN Red List of Threatened Species, version 2014.2, 2013. http://www.iucnredlist.org/details/39049/0

Mayntz, Melissa. "Why Birds Migrate." http://birding.about.com/od/birdbehavior/a/Why-Birds-Migrate.htm

McPherson, Angie. "Rare Pictures: Snow Leopards Caught in Camera Trap." *National Geographic*, January 25, 2014. http://news.nationalgeographic.com/news/2014/01/140125-snow-leopard-pakistan-animals-science-world-endangered-species/

Mech, L.D., and L. Boitani. "*Canis lupis*." The IUCN Red List of Threatened Species, 2010, Version 2014.3. http://www.iucnredlist.org/details/3746/0

WORKS CONSULTED

Mech, L. David, and Luigi Boitani, editors. *Wolves: Behavior, Ecology, and Conservation*. Chicago: The University of Chicago Press, 2003.

Mech, L. David. "The Challenge of Wolf Recovery." *Wildlife Society News*, March 22, 2013. http://news.wildlife.org/featured/the-challenge-of-wolf-recovery/

Montsion, Leah. "*Uncia uncia*: Snow Leopard." *Animal Diversity Web*, University of Michigan Museum of Zoology, 2014. http://animaldiversity.org/accounts/Uncia_uncia/

Myers, Vanessa Richins. "What is a Krummholz?" http://treesandshrubs.about.com/od/treeshrubbasics/f/What-Is-A-Krummholz.htm

Naish, Darren. "A New Living Species of Large Mammal: Hello, *Tapirus kabomani*!" *Scientific American*, December 17, 2013. http://blogs.scientificamerican.com/tetrapod-zoology/2013/12/17/new-living-species-of-tapir/

Naqvi, Hassan. "Saving Snow Leopards." *Express Tribune*, February 16, 2014. http://tribune.com.pk/story/672403/saving-snow-leopards/

National Audubon Society. "Red-Naped Sapsucker Sphyrapicus nuchalis." http://birds.audubon.org/birds/red-naped-sapsucker

National Geographic. "Wolf: *Canis lupus*." http://animals.nationalgeographic.com/animals/mammals/wolf/

Nechvatal, Natalie. "*Tapirus pinchaque*, Mountain Tapir." University of Michigan Museum of Zoology, *Animal Diversity Web*, 2001. http://animaldiversity.org/accounts/Tapirus_pinchaque/

Roady, Laura. "Baby Animals Can Be Born Helpless or Ready to Follow Mom." *Bonners Ferry Herald*, May 3, 2012. http://www.bonnersferryherald.com/local/article_85b44f3c-955d-11e1-9a0d-0019bb2963f4.html

San Diego Zoo Animals. "Tapir: Odds and Ends Make a Magnificent Beast." http://animals.sandiegozoo.org/animals/tapir

Schaming, Taza. "Importance of Whitebark Pines and Clark's Nutcrackers in Western Ecosystems." *American Forests*. http://www.americanforests.org/our-programs/endangered-western-forests/importance-of-whitebark-pines-and-clarks-nutcrackers-in-western-ecosystems/

Shapiro, Leo. "*Sphyrapicus nuchalis*, Red-naped Sapsucker: Brief Summary." *Encyclopedia of Life*. http://eol.org/pages/1047045/details

Snow Leopard Conservancy. "Threats To Snow Leopard Survival." http://snowleopardconservancy.org/threats-to-snow-leopard-survival/

Snow Leopard Trust. "A Year in the Life." http://www.snowleopard.org/learn/cat-facts/a-year-in-the-life

Snow Leopard Trust. "Habitat." http://www.snowleopard.org/learn/cat-facts/habitat

Snow Leopard Trust. "Snow Leopard Fact Sheet." http://www.snowleopard.org/downloads/snow_leopard_fact_sheet_english.pdf

State of Utah Natural Resources, Division of Wildlife Resources. "Red-Naped Sapsucker." http://dwrcdc.nr.utah.gov/rsgis2/search/SearchSelection.asp?Group=AVES&Species=VERT

US Fish and Wildlife Service. "News, Information and Recovery Status Reports." Gray Wolves in the Northern Rocky Mountains: Mountain-Prairie Region, September 25, 2014. http://www.fws.gov/mountain-prairie/species/mammals/wolf/

US Fish and Wildlife Service. "Whitebark Pine." Endangered Species: Mountain-Prairie Region, April 10, 2014. http://www.fws.gov/mountain-prairie/species/plants/whitebarkpine/

Wegge, Per, Rinjan Shrestha, and Øystein Flagstad. "Snow Leopard *Panthera uncia* Predation on Livestock and Wild Prey in a Mountain Valley in Northern Nepal: Implications for Conservation Management." *Wildlife Biology*, June 2012, pp. 131-141. http://www.bioone.org/doi/pdf/10.2981/11-049

Western Wildlife Outreach. "Wolf Biology and Behavior." http://westernwildlife.org/gray-wolf-outreach-project/biology-behavior-4/

Whitebark Pine Ecosystem Foundation. "Threats: Why We Are Concerned About the Future of Whitebark Pine." http://whitebarkfound.org/?page_id=52

Whitebark Pine Ecosystem Foundation. "Why Whitebark Pine Matters." http://whitebarkfound.org/?page_id=22

Wolf Park. "Wolves." http://wolfpark.org/animals/info/wolves/

World Wildlife Foundation. "Snow Leopard." http://wwf.panda.org/what_we_do/endangered_species/snow_leopard/

Zoological Society of London. Edge: Evolutionarily Distinct & Globally Endangered. Mammals. "75. Mountain Tapir (*Tapirus pinchaque*)." http://www.edgeofexistence.org/mammals/species_info.php?id=80

FURTHER READING

Brandenburg, Jim and Judy. *Face To Face With Wolves*. Washington, DC: National Geographic, 2010.

Montgomery, Sy. *Saving the Ghost of the Mountain: An Expedition Among Snow Leopards in Mongolia*. New York: Houghton Mifflin, 2009.

Raatma, Lucia. *Snow Leopards*. New York: Children's Press, 2013.

ON THE INTERNET

National Geographic: Red-Naped Sapsucker
http://animals.nationalgeographic.com/animals/birding/red-naped-sapsucker/

National Park Service: WebRangers
http://www.nps.gov/webrangers/

National Wildlife Federation Kids: Clark's Nutcracker
http://www.nwf.org/Kids/Ranger-Rick/Animals/Birds/Clarks-Nutcracker.aspx

PBS NOVA: What's In a Howl?
http://www.pbs.org/wgbh/nova/wolves/howl.html

San Diego Zoo Animals: Tapir
http://animals.sandiegozoo.org/animals/tapir

GLOSSARY

adapt (uh-DAPT)—to adjust to a change in conditions or environment

ancestor (AN-ses-ter)—a family member from whom a person or animal descends, such as a grandparent, great-grandparent, etc.

cache (KASH)—a hiding place, especially in the ground

camouflage (KAM-uh-flahzh)—an appearance that is used to hide an animal from its enemies

cavity (KAV-i-tee)—a hollow space or hole

chuff (CHUHF)—a puffing sound like a steam engine

conservation (kon-ser-VEY-shuhn)—saving from injury or loss

courtship (KOHRT-ship)—behavior in animals that occurs before and during mating

crown—a tree's leaves and branches

disperse (dih-SPURS)—to scatter something in various directions

ecosystem (EE-koh-sis-tuhm)—a system of interaction of the plants and animals in a community

elevation (el-uh-VEY-shuhn)—the height of a place above sea level

excavate (EKS-kuh-veyt)—to make a hole by digging or scooping to remove material

fertilizer (FUR-tl-ahy-zer)—a substance that adds nutrients to the soil, helping plants to grow

fungus (FUHNG-guhs)—a life form that lives by breaking down living material such as wood; yeast, molds, and mushrooms are fungi

gestation (je-STEY-shuhn)—the length of time of pregnancy

habitat (HAB-i-tat)—the natural environment that a plant or animal lives in

hybrid (HAHY-brid)—the plant or animal that is produced by the mating of two animals or plants of different breeds or species

litter (LIT-er)—a group of babies that an animal has at the same birth

nape (neyp)—the back of the neck

nutrient (NOO-tree-uhnt)—substance that promotes life and good health in the body, particularly in food

pelt—the raw hide or skin of an animal

poacher (POH-cher)—a person who hunts an animal illegally, usually by trespassing on private or protected land

range—the area that a species lives in; also home range—the area that a specific animal or group of animals considers its home area and usually stays within

regionally extinct (REE-juh-nl-ee ik-STINGKT)—no longer existing in a specific area

regurgitated (ri-GUR-ji-teyt-ed)—vomited or brought back up through the mouth (food that has been partially digested)

snout—the part of an animal's head that contains its nose and jaws

solitary (SOL-i-ter-ee)—living alone

stunted (STUHN-tid)—slowed or stopped growth

tundra (TUHN-druh)—the flat, treeless plain biome that exists in the arctic areas of North America, Europe, and Asia

INDEX

About the Author

Bonnie Hinman has loved studying nature since she was a child growing up on her family's farm. Today she is a certified Missouri Master Naturalist and works in her community educating children and adults about the natural world around them. She also volunteers her time to restore and maintain the local ecosystem. Hinman has had more than thirty books published including Mitchell Lane's *Threat to the Leatherback Turtle*. She lives with her husband Bill in Joplin, Missouri, near her children and five grandchildren.